D1583142

'Dublin's legendary, lofty, clattery café,'
was the phrase used by the celebrated American
cookery expert Ken Hom to describe Bewley's in
the international food and drink section of the

Courvoisier Book of the Best
(London 1988).

THE LEGENDARY LOFTY CLATTERY CAFÉ

Bewley's OF IRELAND

TONY FARMAR

First published in 1988 by
Riversend Ltd.,
19/20 Fleet Street,
Dublin 2.
Tel: (01) 776761

Text © Tony Farmar 1988

All rights reserved

ISBN 0-9514022-0-X

Cover illustrations: Pauline Bewick
Design: Ger Garland
Typesetting: Printset & Design Ltd.
Printed in Ireland by Microprint

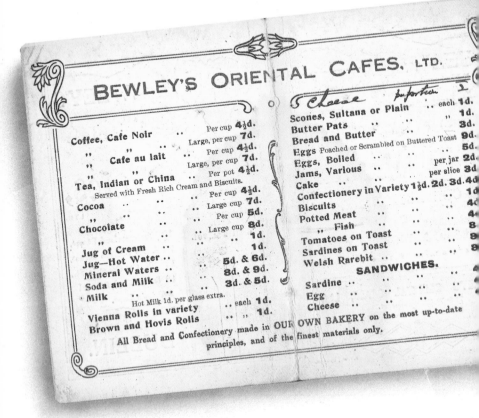

A menu from the 1930s.

CONTENTS

ARMS OF THE BEWLEYS OF CUMBERLAND.

as confirmed to Sir Edmund Thomas Bewley by Ulster King of Arms.

BEWLEYS

Bewleys is the heart and the hearth of Dublin. There is a sense in which Dubliners behave like a large, sometimes unruly family; and walking into Bewleys never fails to give me the feeling that I am stepping into a home. This is quite irrational and therefore, for me at least, totally believable. And it is a pleasure to be able to become part of that family merely by dropping in for a coffee and a shiny bun or two. Bewleys is cosy without being complacent, comfortable without being soporific. There is a special Bewley buzz that is both stimulating and reassuring. In the faces, one always finds a pleasant mixture of strangeness and familiarity. The atmosphere is full of a lovely rattling music made up of cups and chatter, gossip and laughter, watchful eyes and gadabout tongues.

Bewleys is brown. I'm sure there are lots of other colours but brown is the colour I think of when Bewleys pops into my head in a foreign land. Wherever I go I am always visited by this brown Bewleys. Nowhere on earth is quite like it. It is friendly, warm, lively and zippydoo. In the winter, when Bewleys is damp, it has lots of extra interesting smells. You have to jostle a bit, I notice, during winter. But the man who doesn't enjoy a bit of Bewleyjostling should be sentenced to some other kind of coffee.

Dublin would not be Dublin without Bewleys. My own response to it is quite simple: I love the place.

Brendan Kennelly

CHAPTER ONE

The Tea Trade

For three generations Bewley's Oriental Cafés have had a special place in the hearts of Dubliners. Shoppers and gossipers, actors, poets, students, politicians, lovers and business people, townees and country people, tramps and tourists all make time in their day for half an hour or so on the famous red plush benches. People come to Bewley's to see and be seen; to savour a moment's leisure, or a little sugared luxury, in the unique mix of private and public space provided by the high ceilings and cloistered booths, in a nostalgic atmosphere of open fires and mahogany.

They come for a leisurely breakfast with the newspapers; for lunch with friends; for business meetings or deep conversation over sticky buns and tea; or simply for a refreshing cuppa, amid the friendly clatter of crockery, and the fierce smell of roasting coffee that spills into Dublin's central shopping streets.

Bewley's is the Irish counterpart of those great cafés that spread through Europe after the first introduction of coffee in the seventeenth century. In serious-minded England coffee houses developed into financial institutions such as Lloyds and the stock exchange, or became places for political intrigue. In Venice, Florian's in the Piazza di San Marco, and in Paris, Procope's, were the rendezvous of the idle, of gossips, conversationalists, wits and beautiful people. Everywhere the cafés became centres of social life — clubs without an entrance fee that generated an extraordinary affection and loyalty among their patrons.

Since Bewley's first café opened in a busy Dublin street nearly a hundred years ago, the famous and the infamous have enjoyed this atmosphere: James Joyce discussed the setting-up of Ireland's first cinema in Bewley's, and Arthur Griffith, Paddy Kavanagh, Maud Gonne, Jimmy O'Dea, Micheal MacLiammoir, Mary Lavin, Terry Wogan and Ludwig Wittgenstein, to name only a few, all visited the cafés regularly. Up from the country for shopping? An essential part of the treat was a visit to Bewley's for tea. Books were talked out of existence, political plots dissected, business plans hatched, tea-

A companionable cup of Bewley's tea, in Westmoreland Street café.

time treats dispensed, gossip exchanged (*'Well! As I said at the time ...'*).

Bewley's now run five cafés, seven shops, and several franchising units, serving some 45,000 customers a week. Over 200 staff contribute to a turnover of £10 million, deriving from the cafés, from wholesale supplies of coffee and tea, and from retail sales of a range of products from jam to wine, but particularly their own famous bakery goods. These pages describe how the company developed from quite small beginnings in the China tea business, to an institution that Garret Fitzgerald, when he was Taoiseach, described as *'an integral and vital part of Dublin's essential character and atmosphere'*.

The cornerstone of all Bewley's business is the Irish appetite for the products of two exotic shrubs originally found only in China and Africa: *Camellia sinensis* and *Coffea arabica*. Tea and coffee are so much part of our way of life now, that it is impossible to imagine Ireland without them. Yet a mere 150 years ago they were virtually unknown to ordinary people, being drunk only by the gentry. The companies run by the Bewley family, of which Bewley's Cafés are the only survivors, were intimately involved in developing the Irish taste for tea and later for coffee.

The Bewley family is French in origin; they moved from France to the north of England in the middle ages, first to Yorkshire and then to Cumberland, where they were in the fourteenth century. During the religious turmoil of the seventeenth century some members of the family became 'by convincement' members of the Society of Friends (Quakers) under the influence of the fiery George Fox.

What differentiated Quakers from other radical sects of the day was the doctrine of the *Inner Light*. Fox described this as the *'mystical, but Divine, light in the hearts of men; a light which would, if followed honestly and steadily, infallibly lead to God: and that without the aid of either the Bible or any ordinances'*. Every act, grave or trivial, was to be judged according to this light of truth. The stubbornly maintained assertion that a person's inward truth should have more weight than the Bible or the statements of the Church often got members of the new sect into trouble with the authorities.

In 1700 Mungo Bewley, the first of the family to live in Ireland, came to the midlands at the age of 23, to practice his religion and seek a living in a more tolerant and less strictly policed atmosphere. The family thrived, specialising in the wool and other clothing trades. By 1780 Mungo II (grandson of the first Mungo) had a linen factory in Mountrath

Above left: Samuel Bewley (1764-1837) began the family involvement with tea and coffee. His great, great, grandson Patrick Bewley, above, carries on the family tradition.

employing as many as 150 people. His brother, John Bewley, had a textile printing works near Blessington in County Wicklow, and a third brother, Samuel, had set himself up in Dublin as a silk merchant, importing silk from Italy, the Levant and London.

Samuel was born in 1764, the son of Thomas Bewley and his wife Susanna Pim. She was a member of the great Pim family that was to become powerful throughout the nineteenth century in Dublin financial and business circles. As we shall see, Samuel was frequently to be joined with his Pim cousins in financial ventures.

By the 1820s Samuel was a great man in Dublin commercial circles. He was a ship-owner; he was Treasurer of the Chamber of Commerce;

he was a major shareholder (with Joseph R. Pim) in the Mining Company of Ireland (capital £500,000); he was a leading founder and honorary auditor of the National Assurance Company (capital £1 million), which was among other things for twenty years the only Irish company undertaking marine insurance; he inaugurated the Dublin Savings Bank, which by 1838 had three branches in the city; he was a major investor in a Quaker-owned brewery (the temperance lines were not then so strictly drawn). He was also the prime influence in the establishment of the Retreat at Bloomfield in Donnybrook, the first asylum in Ireland to insist on the gentle treatment of the insane.

Many of Samuel's business contacts and partners were Quakers, and the ideals of the Society of Friends have been a significant influence in the development of the firm ever since. In 1820 there were no more than 700 Quakers in Dublin, out of a total city population of 224,000. They came from some 130 families, who were in general well-off and closely connected to each other, a connection they took pains to preserve. Children were expected to marry within the fold, on pain of expulsion from the Society. A closely-knit series of family and business alliances grew up, of which the Pims and the Bewleys were among the most prominent.

Following the implications of the doctrine of inward truth, Quakers became famous for providing in all their commercial dealings fair measure, reasonable prices and good quality. The Quakers were also well-known in business circles for their attitude to bankruptcy, of which they strongly disapproved. Because the banking and company law systems were so underdeveloped, businesses at this time were run by a web of interlocking personal credit and loans. If one merchant house got into trouble, it frequently brought others down as well, by breaking the chain of owing and paying. Although this might have happened without any personal fault, Quakers held that not to pay one's debts was an offence against truth, and expelled members from the Society if they failed in business.

To prevent this, if it was discovered that one of their number was in difficulties, certain Friends, selected for their sensitivity and knowledge of commercial procedures, would be appointed to help him. A report on the case would be brought in to the next monthly meeting. This would describe the general outlines of the case, and unless there was any flagrant transgression of the customary laws of the Society the visitors would be encouraged to continue their 'care' of the transgressor and report back to a further meeting and so on for a number of months. The object of the procedure was to ensure that the transgressor would act according to the demands of the Quaker view of justice in the payment of debts. Samuel Bewley frequently acted as advisor on these occasions.

Despite Samuel Bewley's success in other areas, his silk business was not prospering. Fashions had changed after the French Revolution, so that men no longer wore silk stockings; and economic changes after the Act of Union meant that more and more Irish trade was being taken by London merchants. Samuel spread his wings, and began trading in other goods, particularly from the Mediterranean. In November 1824 he advertised for sale in the *Dublin Mercantile Advertiser* the following goods: gum arabic, opium (for medicinal purposes), galls, liquorice paste, Gallipoli oil, silkworm gut and Turkey carpets. As an afterthought he mentioned that he had in stock 1,500 drums of new Turkey figs, and 60 tons of valonia.

Samuel had been pushing the Chamber of Commerce for some time to encourage the direct importation of goods into Dublin, no doubt conscious that failure to do this had been a major cause of the silk industry's collapse. In 1835 his enterprising son Charles (who died young) engineered the great coup of importing 2,099 chests of tea on the *Hellas*, which was said to be the first ship ever freighted directly from Canton to Dublin; a few months later the *Mandarin* loaded a further 8,623 chests. These two consignments between them probably accounted for 40 per cent of the annual Irish consumption of tea at that time (though of course some of it may have been intended for export to England).

This activity, as a contemporary in the tea-trade put it, *'caused a complete revolution in the old-fashioned style of business in that article ...'*. At this time all tea was grown in China, and until recently every ounce had been sold in the East India Company's auction rooms in the City of London. In 1833 the statutory monopoly of the East India Company was broken; merchants could make their own arrangements, and tea suddenly began to be imported direct into Dublin, Liverpool, Belfast and Cork. Tea was to remain Bewley's key product for years, only to be overtaken by coffee in the new century.

There were various grades of tea, distinguished by exotic names which have now fallen out of use: gunpowder, caper, bohea, congou, singlo, twankay. At this time the Irish consumed a mere half a pound of tea a head per year, and, if we can judge from the contents of that first shipment in the *Hellas*, drank mainly the better-quality congous and pekoes — only 15 per cent of the consignment was the low-grade bohea.

The one thing all teas had in common was their expense. The duty on a pound of congou was 2s 2d, effectively 125 per cent. Like alcohol today, tea was a major contributor to government revenues. The duty on tea paid for nearly two-thirds of the whole of the (admittedly small) British civil service establishment, including the expenses of the Crown.

Samuel Bewley died in 1837, leaving seven of his thirteen children alive after him. Youngest of these was Joshua, the direct founder of the business we know today as Bewley's, who was only eighteen. By this time the Bewleys had built up a network of related businesses in Dublin. Samuel's brother Henry ran an apothecary and chemist establishment

BELL'S LIFE

AND SPORTIN

Price Seven Pence.]—SUNDAY, MARCH 1, 1835.

at Eton, acci-	ARRIVAL OF A SHIP DIRECT FROM CHINA AT KINGSTOWI
ymptoms from	On Saturday week the first vessel which has ever sailed to Ire
{ of the first	from China arrived at Kingstown, laden with teas, the property
' at the town	the Messrs. Bewley, of William-street, and called the Hellas, c
	manded by Captain Scanlan.

Bell's Life in London and Sporting Chronicle *reporting the first Irish shipment of China tea.*

in Sackville (O'Connell) Street called Bewley and Evans; Joshua's brother James was a tea and wine merchant in Dun Laoghaire, and the eldest son Joseph ran Samuel Bewley and Sons, an importing merchant, from William Street.

It is likely that Joshua began his commercial career with Joseph, who soon became prominent in organising help for victims of the Famine. In November 1846 a group of Friends, led by Jonathan Pim and Joseph Bewley, formed the Central Relief Committee, which pioneered the organisation of soup kitchens and food shipments to areas badly hit by the potato blight. The dedicated work of this committee in developing famine relief services was one of the few bright spots in those dark days. Close connections with American and British Friends were very important in this effort. American Quakers, for instance, provided nearly two-thirds of all Quaker relief supplies during the Famine period.

Joshua set up his own business as a tea merchant some time in the 1840s. A decade later he worked from 19 and 20 Sycamore Alley, where were based his China Tea Company, the store-room of Samuel Bewley & Sons, and a depot for his uncle Henry's other business Bewley, Fisher & Co. Sycamore Alley (now Sycamore Street) runs down from Dame Street, near the Olympia Theatre, to Essex Street.

Then as now, that area of Dublin is more remarkable for traders, bankers and administrators than shops and retailing. Sycamore Alley itself was not at all grand: at number 1 (from the Dame Street end) lived Charles Keenan, a dealer in leeches for medical use, and eight of the houses were in tenements and a further four in ruins. The new business was however significantly near to the handsome Quaker meeting house in Eustace Street, which Samuel Bewley had been instrumental in developing.

IN LONDON,

CHRONICLE.

inued the learned lexicographer, " who discovers a medicine to alleviate
orments deserves well of his country ; but he who can effect a cure should
: a monument raised to his memory as high as St. Paul's, as wide as the
nes, and as lasting as eternity." The success of Blair's Go
c Pills, in the eradication of those formidable plagues, i
over r of so invaluable and efficacious a remed t
iflicted.

above all
by C

Joshua was reasonably prosperous by 1850: apart from his tea merchanting he also did some business as an actuary, and owned a fine house in 20 Pembroke Road, only two doors away from the Director of the Irish Geological Survey. His brothers, who appear to have been considerably better off, had houses in the comfortable suburbs of south Dublin, in Sandford Hill, Ranelagh (now occupied by Gonzaga College), in Rockville, Blackrock and in Rathfarnham.

Unfortunately no records have survived to reveal the scale of Joshua's tea business, or indeed how his business was run. His will of 1866 mentions a stable of horses in Coghill's court, between Eustace Street and Sycamore Alley, which opened under an arch into Dame Street. He was certainly in at the beginning of a growing market. Between 1840 and 1890 the Irish diet changed radically. In particular the tea-drinking habit, combined with a taste for sugar and white bread, spread rapidly westward throughout the country after the Famine. Annual tea consumption grew from 4.1 million lbs in 1840 to 35 million lbs in 1890.

For generations before this the Irish diet had been much as Sir William Petty described it in 1672: 'the diet of the people is milk, sweet and sour, thick and thin ... their food is bread in cakes, potatoes from August til May, eggs and butter'. Two hundred years later, An tAthair Peadar Ó Laoghaire recalled 'the oatmeal bread and the wheaten bread from the mill, hen-eggs and duck-eggs, sweet milk and thick milk and buttermilk, the potatoes and butter taken fresh from the churn, the bit of bacon now and again' that he used to eat as a young man on holidays from Maynooth in the 1860s.

But change was in the air. The failure of the potato crops during the Famine had introduced new dietary habits into the country, in particular the much-disliked maize. This was eaten as stirabout, a form of porridge made by boiling it in water to the consistency of a soft pudding and then mixing with sugar and milk. A government enquiry in 1864 found that sugar was used by 80 per cent of the population (usually with maize

PRODU

GROW

80 TEA BAGS
Bewley's

Bewley's
OF IRELAND
IRISH
BREAKFAST
TEA
4 OZ NET WT 113g
The most popular of our teas
Pure Indian tea

CLIPPER CLASS

Tea

Bewley's
OF IRELAND
IRISH
AFTERNOON
TEA
4 OZ NET WT 113g
A blend of African and Indian teas

Bewley's
OF IRELAND
EARL
GREY
TEA
NET WT 113g
ed with Oil of Bergamot

Irish **Bewley's**
OF IRELAND
Breakfast
Tea
NET WT. 125 g. (4.4 oz)

Bewley's
IRELAND

AS CREATED OUT
N IN THE SPARKLING
NURTURED BY NAT
RAY AND FLOWING
FORM AMIDST
CUP IS AN ENLIVE
OF DELIVERING STRE
OUR TO MATCH EVE

Bewley's
OF IRELAND
Assam Tea
113g.

Bewley's
OF IRELAND
Darjeeling Tea

Bewley's

*A*fter 150 years, Bewley's
still import and pack their
own distinctive tea blends.

Bewley's are brand leaders in quality teas and coffees.

I Joshua Bewley of Bray in the County of Wicklow and of Sycamore Alley in the City of Dublin Merchant do make publish and declare this to be my last Will and Testament, and I hereby revoke all wills heretofore made by me. Whereas I am possessed of certain houses and Concerns in Sycamore Alley aforesaid and in Coghills Court in the City of Dublin wherein I carry on my trade and business of a Tea Merchant, and I am also possessed of certain premises situate at Novara Avenue in the Town of Bray aforesaid wherein I reside,— Now I give devise and bequeath to my Trustees hereinafter named all my said property in the City of Dublin and at Bray and all other my estate and effects both real and personal upon the trusts hereinafter declared Concerning the same, that is to say:— As to my said houses and premises in Sycamore Alley & Coghills Court and all my Stock in trade trade and other fixtures and all Machinery and implements which may be in and upon the said premises, horses, Carts and drays and other Carriages used in my business at the time of my death upon trust to manage and carry on

1

on

and therefore not in the potato season), tea by only 57 per cent. Tea was, so a witness reported, *'used very generally in towns, and sometimes to a large extent, whilst in some of the country places its use is almost unknown.'*

Gradually the habit took on throughout the country. Many people no doubt picked up the taste for tea while working as servants in the houses of the gentry. An early example of this comes from the diary of Elizabeth Smith of Baltiboys, Co Wicklow, who records having tremendous trouble with a newly-recruited servant. At the bottom of it was, as she wrote crossly in her diary, *'the wish to have tea for her breakfast like the other maids! She, who has often and often had but one meal a day and that dry potatoes.'*

One contributory cause to the spread of tea was the temperance movement, itself allied to a general spread of refinement throughout the century that made such rougher traditions as Donnybrook Fair, faction fights and the drunken revelling described by both Joshua Barrington and Humphrey O'Sullivan no longer acceptable. Strong drink was also held by many nationalists to have contributed to the failure of the risings in 1798.

As a result of all these forces, Irish tea consumption began to rise very markedly. Between 1840 and 1860 it went up three-fold to just under 2 lbs per head per annum; by 1900 it had risen to 7.5 lbs per head, not far away from the present figure. The steady reduction in tax over this period, from 2s 2d per pound in 1850 to 4d per pound in 1880 was no doubt a considerable help.

By 1870 Joshua's business occupied five houses, nos 15-19 Sycamore Alley, and his brothers and cousins had similarly extended themselves into a considerable range of businesses. His brother Thomas ran a sugar refinery in Brunswick (now Pearse) Sreet, and *his* son, also Thomas, ran the shipbuilders Bewley, Webb & Co. Joshua's brother William was running Fawcett & Co., 18-20 Henry Street, which by the 1880s was renamed Bewley, Sons & Co. and was the biggest wine and whiskey retailer in Dublin. Joshua himself had moved twelve miles out of town to the fashionable resort of Bray, where he lived in a comfortable house under the shadow of Bray Head.

CHAPTER TWO

Into The Café Business

The tea habit, as we have seen, spread rapidly throughout Ireland from 1860 onwards. As happened in many other places in the world, mildly addictive stimulants (such as tea, coffee, tobacco, betel or cola-nut) proved so popular in all walks of life that venerated food habits were quickly dropped in their favour. At first distribution was a problem, as the Irish retail trade wasn't very well developed. So a combination of direct deliveries from merchant houses such as Bewley's, and a system of travelling tea salesmen, spread the new drink. And it wasn't just any old tea. The Irish tea drinker insisted on good quality — *'the poorest of the population of Ireland now ... buy the finest tea'* announced one expert in 1885. *'A country woman in Ireland prefers to pay 4d an ounce for tea; and she will get such tea as you do not get in a London hotel.'*

Perhaps the reason for the preference for good quality tea was that many people first discovered tea in the well-stocked kitchens of the Big House. There was also a common habit of letting it stew for considerable periods. As one inspector of the Congested Districts Board in Donegal reported in the 1890s, *'tea is taken to an extent which their means do not warrant, by both better-off families and the poorest. Children and adults alike drink it. The tea is boiled or stewed for about half an hour before it is taken ...'*

By then tea was being drunk three or four times a day even in the very poorest districts of the West. Some families were spending up to a sixth of the household income on tea and sugar. (In 1980 the average Irish household spent less than 1 per cent of its income on these commodities.) In the country the housewife would often barter eggs or knitting-work for tea, though the exchange rate was not always fair, as a contemporary journalist noted: *'the price fixed by the egg collector was 6d. per dozen; its value in tea or sugar was delivered instead. Two ounces of tea or one pound of sugar was the equivalent substitute for the 6d. These commodities, valued at current retail prices were worth 2¾d or at most 3d.'*

Faced with this rapid increase in consumption, doctors began to suggest that the habit of drinking large quantities of long-

The famous Harry Clarke windows in the Grafton Street café.

South Great George's Street in 1910; Bewley's first café, at No. 13, was a few doors up on the right.

stewed tea, combined with a poor diet, contributed to rates of mental illness. *'Tea drinking is becoming a curse,'* wrote Dr Moore of Letterkenny, *'the people are developing a craving for tea just as great as that which a drunkard has for alcohol.'*

In the 1870s, towards the end of his life, Joshua Bewley left the houses in Sycamore Alley and moved to 11 (later renumbered to 13) South Great George's Street, and the firm traded under the name of his elder son Charles (named after his enterprising uncle). The move was no doubt prompted by the promotion of major development plans for the George's Street/Dame Street area. In 1876 a substantial road (which was of course

The South City Market, completed in 1881, was Ireland's first purpose built shopping centre.

never built) was proposed parallel to Dame Street, to run straight from Christchurch Place, between the Castle and the City Hall, to join George's Street just south of Dame Lane. This would have left Sycamore Alley very much in a backwater. At the same time it was being suggested that the Castle itself was hardly impressive enough for its function, and that one of the buildings on St. Stephen's Green should be adapted for the purpose.

More concretely, a group of George's Street businessmen had just in 1876 achieved the passage of a private Act of Parliament to develop South Great George's Street itself. The great department store of Pim, Brothers and other major-traders in the street, such as Dockrell's, discovered that shoppers were increasingly being attracted towards fashionable Grafton Street shops in preference to George's Street. To remedy this, and to develop the area generally, they set up the South City Market Company

Bewley's much loved cakes and pastries are still served in their cafés and shops.

This Wedgewood tea-pot, now in the Bewley Museum, was for years used in the cafés.

to build a major indoor market and shopping centre in the middle of George's Street.

They had first to widen all the streets around the site (George's Street itself, Exchequer Street, Drury Street and Fade Street) to their present dimensions. In the process they purchased and closed as many as twelve private slaughter-houses and pulled down numerous houses which had been described as unfit for human habitation. The result, the South City Market as we know it today, was finally opened in 1881. Unfortunately this early shopping centre development was not a success, perhaps because (as the *Irish Builder* reported in 1882) the whole idea was based on English models, and English architects and workmen had been largely employed in the construction, to the resentment of the Dubliners.

After a lively start in 1835 by Joshua's brother Charles, the Dublin tea market had gradually, over a period of thirty years, subsided into dependence on London. Thomas Keyler, a fellow tea trader, put it thus: *'had Charles Bewley lived, it would have been very different ... but he left few behind him, and those having money left them by their fathers, clutched it, and let their establishments sink down to the position of mere wholesale grocers.'*

In 1891 Findlater's, who claimed to have been the first to import Indian tea into Ireland, noted in their popular women's journal *The Lady of the House* that China tea had dropped in ten years from three-quarters of the market to less than 40 per cent. Their prices were identical for both types, ranging from 3s 2d for a pound of Extra Quality to 1s 6d for Good and Strong. (A skilled bricklayer was then paid 8d a hour for a 54 hour week.)

Simultaneously with the change in origin, tea had become one of the first mass market branded goods. Firms such as Brooke Bond, Liptons and Denshams (with their famous brand Mazawattee) spent fortunes advertising branded pre-packed teas, which had very often been grown on the firm's own plantations. These radical changes in the tea market must have considerably worsened the position of a small wholesaler (particularly one specialising in China tea), and may well have prompted the Bewleys' decision to move across Dame Street and concentrate on the shop side of their business.

Just before the move, Joshua's second son Ernest Bewley, the eventual progenitor of Bewley's Oriental Cafés, began to work in Charles Bewley and Co, tea and coffee merchants, at the age of sixteen. His pay was 1/- a week, all found, including his daily fare from Bray. Things were not then in a vigorous way of business. Ernest is remembered as saying afterwards that he *'never had any success until he got into number 13 South Great George's Street.'* The Bewleys had to work hard to build up the shop's trade in tea, sugar, small amounts of coffee and oriental decorative goods. They often worked late into Saturday night to supply demand.

Dublin was at this time a city of just over 300,000 inhabitants. In the older area of the city, inside the canals, the population had hardly grown at all for forty years, and was housed in the now rapidly decaying houses of the departed gentry. The middle-classes had retreated from the city centre to the fast-growing suburbs of Rathmines and Rathgar, Pembroke, Blackrock and Clontarf. Not only was the newly built housing specially designed for nineteenth century living, but the self-administered townships offered a chance to avoid the social problems, industrial decline and distress of the city. Rates were cheaper, too. By 1891 nearly a quarter of the population of the metropolitan area lived in these suburbs.

Offices, fashionable shops, mercantile warehouses and professional rooms, however, tended to remain in the inner area. As a result many people travelled regularly into town, and public transport services sprang up to meet this demand — railways, trams (electrification began in 1896, and was complete by 1901), and a great variety of horse-drawn vehicles. The bicycling craze had just been given a new lease of life by the invention in 1888 of the pneumatic tyre, by Dubliner John Boyd Dunlop; this put a comfortable cushion of air between the rough roads and the cyclist.

The most startling innovation was the motor car, which first came onto the streets of Dublin in the late 1890s. It was of course at first a rich man's plaything — a typical car such as a Humber cost £275, or nearly three times a workingman's annual income — and by April 1904 only 58 cars had been registered in Dublin. Ten years later cars were available on the market for £100, and 1500 were registered in the city.

Once in town, whether for shopping or work, the residents of the

Ireland's first cinema, the Volta in Mary Street; its manager was James Joyce, here pictured by Augustus John.

suburbs needed somewhere to refresh themselves. The characters in *Ulysses* have the choice of several pubs, coffee stalls, the DBC (officially the Dublin Bakery Co. where, as the wags said, Damn Bad Cakes were to be had) and eating houses such as that in Duke Street, which revolted even the unfastidious Bloom. *'He pushed in the door of the Burtons restaurant. Stink gripped his trembling breath: pungent meatjuice, slop of greens. See the animals feed. Men, men, men. Perched on high stools by the bar, hats shoved back, at the tables calling for more bread no charge, swilling, wolfing gobfuls of sloppy food, their eyes bulging, wiping wetted moustaches...''.*

Charles Bewley left Ireland for health reasons in the 1890s. He settled in Tasmania, leaving Ernest Bewley, Joshua's second son, in charge of the business. Ernest, a tall active man, had been tempted at one stage to go into poultry farming. On Charles's departure his undoubted entrepreneurial skills were allowed to flower in the family business. In 1890 he took out an insurance policy, on the stock and fixtures and fittings, which give us an interesting picture of the George's Street premises at the time.

The total insured value was £800, of which £500 was for *'stock in trade held by him ... in his shop and warehouse being the basement and ground floor of ... 13 George's Street.'* There was an additional £300 insurance for trade fixtures and fittings. A note to this last item remarked *'two stoves used for warmth only, are hereby allowed in said premises ... and a coffee roaster, heated and worked by a securely fixed gas engine.'* The value of the stock (which, if he was buying tea at wholesale, we may guess was replaced at least ten times a year on average) enables us to estimate his annual takings at £5,000, or more than fifty times the average skilled wage. Compared to present average wages, this would indicate a turnover of the order of £500,000 today.

There followed a remarkable series of developments which in ten years created a totally new and extremely successful enterprise, the core of the present-day Bewley's. The first step was taken in 1894 when Bewley's first Oriental Café was opened in the George's Street premises. After a family disagreement, Ernest had bought a single consignment of one hundredweight of coffee from a wholesaler, rather than his normal one or two stones from his cousin. In order to stimulate the market for this relatively unknown product, he began to run coffee-making demonstrations at the back of the shop: his wife made scones and buns to go with the coffee, and quite soon it was clear that the idea was extremely popular. Thus was created the unique mix of shops and cafés that Bewley's have held on to ever since.

Two years later, in 1896, the café at 10, Westmoreland Street was opened. (No 12 was bought in 1916 and no 11 was swapped for no 10 in the 1970s.) The menu was simple: tea, coffee, various rolls, rich and often elaborate cakes in the continental style, sticky buns and eggs (boiled, poached or scrambled). Bewley's was primarily a meeting place and a refreshment stop for business people and well-heeled shoppers. It was not a cheap place — Ernest Bewley's motto was *'give the public*

> To C. P. Curran
> 30 August 1904   60 Shelbourne Road.
>
> *My Dear Curran,*
>   *I am in double trouble, mental and material. Can you meet me tomorrow at half past four at smoke-room Bewley's in Westmoreland Street?*
>
>   *Yours truly,*
>   *James Joyce.*

Joyce invites a friend to meet him in Bewley's in Westmoreland Street.

what they want, and let them pay for it'. He was also not inclined to spend money on advertising, relying instead on a top quality image, backed by the rich aroma of roasting coffee that spread through the streets near a Bewley's shop.

The expensive cakes and confectionery items were made by continental specialist bakers (to such a degree that until the Europeans went home or were interned in the Great War, instructions in the bakery were in German). Bewley was extremely clear about the difference between a café and a restaurant, and was firm in maintaining the limit. Increase the size of the menu, he thought, and you simply decrease the return.

This was the café, then quite new, which, as David Norris wrote *'played host at the turn of the century to mid-morning groups of students, at the animated centre of which the young James Joyce was often to be found.'* The Westmoreland Street Bewley's was a regular destination of Joyce's in Dublin: he always had expensive tastes. In an expansive mood over coffee in 1909, he showed a friend a large sum of money he had been given by businessmen to set up a cinema in Dublin. The friend, Richard Best, later librarian of the National Library, refused a loan, and Ireland's first cinema, the Volta in Mary Street, was established with Joyce as manager (it failed soon after).

By 1900 Ernest was doing well enough to be able build himself an elegant new house in the fashionable suburb of Rathgar, with thirty acres of farming land on the River Dodder. That same year he acquired the vacant premises in 19 and 20 Fleet Street. The original idea had been to set up a bicycle shop; unfortunately, so the family legend has it, his partner failed to turn up to a meeting (or perhaps simply proved unreliable), and Ernest, always a stickler for timekeeping, cancelled the arrangement. Fleet Street was made into another café, and in 1905 the premises were rebuilt. Bewley Chambers, with eighteen offices, was built above the café.

Ernest Bewley's watchword was quality: he is remembered as saying *'I want the best of everything, and that's not good enough!'*. He carried this through every part of his life. It is even said (jokingly) that the origin of the famous Jersey herd, which was started in 1903 to supply the growing demand for good quality milk and cream from the cafés, lay in his desire to get the very best manure to nurture his prizewinning

A family group gathered to celebrate Joshua and Margaret Bewley's Golden Wedding in 1895.

sweetpeas. However that may be, the milk and cream from the Jersey cows was of such quality that doctors used to recommend it to their patients.

Very soon after moving to Rathgar, he won the first of a long series of prize medals at the Royal Dublin Society Shows. The first, in 1906, was for the turnout and quality of his delivery vans; this was the beginning of a series of awards that ran on until 1936. The cattle began to win similar prizes in 1912, Bewley's butter in 1920, and his roses in 1907.

In the cafés this competitive search for quality meant that, for instance, only the very best ingredients were used in the cakes and other confectionery items: including pure sugar and butter — the commonly used alternatives of invert sugar and substitute fats were forbidden, at least until the shortages of the Emergency period.

Part of this drive was fuelled by what has been called the almost pedantic honesty of the Quakers. Ernest Bewley certainly insisted that a fair day's work was given for a fair day's pay. John Swift, the bakers' union leader, who worked in Bewley's in the 1920s and early 1930s, remembers that the firm was the first bakery in Dublin to give up night-work; on the other hand, the bakery doors were open for about three minutes after eight o' clock, and then locked. Those who had not arrived by then lost a day's pay. On pilfering too, Bewley's took a strict line. Traditionally bakers regarded a few cakes off the batch as their perks, and in most places nothing would be said. In Bewley's any pilfering was strictly forbidden, a tradition maintained in their time by Ernest's sons.

It is difficult to imagine such a man feeling comfortable in the political atmosphere of Dublin Corporation, which for years had been comprised largely of grocers, publicans, slaughterhouse owners and tenement landlords who used nationalist slogans to conceal inertia and vested interests. Yet in 1907 Bewley was proposed for election to the

Corporation by Lord Ardilaun and various other notables, and won his seat by a convincing majority. A *'splendid victory'*, the staunchly unionist *Irish Times* called it. Bewley was the only Unionist (out of sixty seats) elected for the fifteen wards between the canals. In 1911 he became an Alderman. He resigned in 1914, and his seat was re-taken by the nationalists.

As a Quaker and a Unionist, Bewley's opinions must have been greatly torn during the Great War and the Troubles that followed. The first sign of what these might bring came with great suddenness on Easter Monday 1916, when the Westmoreland Street shop was in the direct line of fire between the Volunteers in O'Connell Street and the students and military sniping from the walls of Trinity.

Ernest Bewley's sympathy with pacifism became practical when he offered John Swift (who had spent two years in English prisons as a conscientious objector) a job in 1919, despite the fact that Swift had previously been sacked from the firm for union activities. But by then pressure of events had forced the company to become a union house, at least in the bakery, and since the disappearance of the Europeans, Bewley's certainly needed skilled bakers. Swift specialised in the confectionery area, moving from rough confectionery (buns, scones, croissants — a popular item — and rolls) to fancy work such as cakes.

It is quite clear that Bewley had no thought of leaving the country, as many rich Protestants did, despite his shrewd estimate of how the new political and economic circumstances would affect his largely Ascendancy and Protestant business clientele. In 1927 he signalled his intention to stay in an unequivocal manner, by opening his most exciting and expensive venture yet, the café in Grafton Street.

Before he did so, he protected the future of the company by incorporating it. He was by now 66, and his eldest son Victor only 14, so this was a desirable move regardless of the Grafton Street development. The Memoranda of the new company stated that the new company took over *'the business now carried on by Ernest Bewley at South Great George's Street and Westmoreland Street, Dublin under the style of Charles Bewley and company ...'*. The three directors are Ernest, his wife Susan and his cousin Thomas Bewley of Sandford Hill, Ranelagh, who was also a director of Jacobs, the biscuit manufacturers. Also on the board was an accountant, Richard Clark, Ernest's brother-in-law, who was to play a crucial role in the survival of the company in later years. There was however no question as to whose company it was: of the 10,000 ''A' Ordinary shares which controlled the voting rights of the company, all but one were held by Ernest or his wife Susan.

The new company had immediately to face two severe challenges: the first being the immense effort of buying and refurbishing the Grafton Street shop, which ten years later was to provide 40 per cent of the company's profits. The second challenge was the long illness and eventual death in 1932 of Ernest Bewley, leaving behind him his twenty-year old son Victor, who had a mere two years' experience of the business.

CHAPTER THREE

Young Mr Victor

The new premises in Grafton Street had a distinguished and interesting history. In the eighteenth century the famous Whyte's Academy, run by the actor and schoolmaster Samuel Whyte, had been located there. Among his pupils were Richard Brinsley Sheridan, Thomas Moore, Robert Emmet and the Duke of Wellington. Ernest Bewley was determined to spare no expense in fitting out the new café. He even commissioned the great stained glass artist Harry Clarke to create the ground floor windows. In March 1927 he reported to the board that he had spent £45,000 in buying and refurbishing the premises, plus a further £14,900 *'largely comprising the cost of ovens, tables, chairs, counters and other café fixtures and fittings'*. The oil-driven ovens quickly proved to be extremely noisy, and had to be replaced. (To put these figures into perspective, the average industrial wage in that year was £2 8s a week, or £126 a year.)

It seems likely that everything may not have been thought out in advance. In August 1926 the *Irish Builder* reported that *'Messrs Millar and Symes have prepared plans for a balcony and a thrust-out lavatory at the premises'*, and in December *'plans have been approved by the City Architect for an additional storey over the bake house at Bewley's café in 78/9 Grafton Street.'* Ernest Bewley appears to have fallen into the expensive trap of developing his building plans as he went along.

By 1928 Bewley was a wealthy man. He was established as Managing Director and Chairman of a thriving company, and he was (privately) landlord of their premises in Westmoreland Street, Fleet Street and Grafton Street. The firm paid him rent for these premises, fixed (at least in the case of Grafton Street) on the advice of an expert from Dockrell's who recommended to the Board *'that the true basis on which the rent should be calculated was 7 per cent on the total cost to the landlord of the premises.'* (The bank rate at this time was 5½ per cent.) His Jersey herd was also a significant source of cream and milk for the firm. The Articles of Association fixed his salary at not less than £2,500 a year, plus 20 per cent commission on pre-tax profits. He also of course received dividends on his shares.

'Dublin can be heaven, with coffee at eleven . . .

Dublin.
Bewley.

FIRE POLICY   SUM INSURED

Nº 1860041   £ 800

NORTHERN ASSURANCE
Company.

ESTABLISHED 1836.

CAPITAL £3,000,000.

PRESENT PREMIUM.   RENEWAL PREMIUM.

£ — : 2 : —   £ — : 16 : —

ONE PENNY 89

Whereas *Ernest Bewley* of *Nº 13, South Great Georges Street, Dublin:* *Tea, Sugar and Coffee Dealer: trading as Messrs. Charles Bewley and Company.*

(hereinafter called the Insured) *has* paid to THE NORTHERN ASSURANCE COMPANY (hereinafter called the Company), the Sum of *Sixteen shillings less a return of fourteen shillings on Policy Nº 141/57/31 hereby cancelled.*

for insuring against Loss or Damage by Fire the Property hereinafter described in the several sums following, viz.:—

£500   *On Stock in Trade, the Insured's own or held by him in trust or on commission, for which he is responsible, contained in his Shop and Warehouse being the basement and ground floor of a Building, brick or stone built and slated or tiled, situate Nº 13, South Great Georges Street aforesaid. The upper portion of building forms part of the Central Hotel.*

300   *On Trade Fixtures, Fittings (excluding Plate Glass and Plate Glass Fronts) and Utensils thereon including Gas Engine & Coffee Roaster &c.*

£800   *Say* **Eight Hundred Pounds**

Memo: Two Stoves used for warmth only, are hereby allowed in said Premises, the flues running into ordinary chimneys, (Warranted that same are securely fixed and free from contact with woodwork) and a Coffee Roaster, heated and worked by a securely fixed gas engine, allowed in basement &c. The Insurance by the last item hereof extends to, and includes said gas engine.

Now the Company hereby agrees with the Insured (but subject to the Terms and Conditions printed on the back hereof, which are to be taken as part of this Policy) that if, the Property above described, or any part thereof, shall be destroyed or damaged by FIRE at any time between the *25th* day of *March* 18*90*, and the *twenty fifth* day of *March* 18*91*, both inclusive, or at any time afterwards, so long as the Insured or his Representatives in Interest shall duly pay to the Company, and it shall accept the sum required for the renewal of this Policy, the Company will out of its Capital, Stock and Funds, pay or make good all such Loss or Damage, to an amount not exceeding in respect of the several matters above specified the sum set opposite thereto respectively (unless previously allowed by Endorsement on the back hereof) and not exceeding in the whole the sum of *Eight Hundred Pounds*

Provided always, and it is hereby agreed that the Capital, Stock and Funds of the Company shall alone be liable to answer and make good all demands under or by virtue of this Policy, and that no Shareholder or Member of the Company shall be liable to any such demands nor be in anywise charged or chargeable by reason of this Policy beyond the amount unpaid on his or her Share or Shares in the Company.

In witness whereof, the Company hath caused its Common Seal to be hereunto affixed at LONDON, the *seventh* day of *May* in the year of our Lord One Thousand Eight Hundred and *Ninety*

Examined

Entered *C&B*

Countersigned

J Robertson

Secretary at Dublin.

Seal of the Company.

Seal No. 482330

(Irish No. 2.)   ☞ Please read the Conditions and examine the Policy, and if incorrect return it immediately to the Office for alteration.

In 1890, Ernest Bewley insured the business for £800.

By using his own money Bewley had provided the firm with a splendid new premises, and one which was to prove immensely valuable in later years. To do this he had taken on himself a large burden of debt, a fact recognised in the relatively high remuneration given to him.

The new premises were however both expensive and troublesome, and when Ernest died in 1932, after a long illness, his health broken down by the difficulties resulting from the building, he left his executors with a debt of £51,000. Since it was not then considered good banking practice to force sales or liquidations, the bank were keen to install an experienced outsider to run the company so that the dividends on Ernest's shares could pay the debt off.

Ernest's eldest son Victor was the obvious family successor, but he was only twenty, and had worked in the firm for just two years. He was moreover an extremely shy man, and drawn to missionary work. However, he was supported by the accountant Richard Clark (Ernest's brother-in-law) and the solicitor, G.A. Overend, the senior partner of A. & L. Goodbody. These two were at the same time the firm's professional advisors, members of the Board and the Trustees of Ernest's estate. Thus encouraged, he agreed to take on the responsibility, and the bank reluctantly accepted the position.

During his stewardship over the next forty years the firm became a much-loved Dublin institution. For most people a lifetime's affection for Bewley's started with childhood treats during shopping expeditions (perhaps after a visit to Santa Claus in one of the department stores); then grew daily as one took lunch or morning coffee from work. Like any club, the regulars became well-known: one pair of businessmen, brothers, met in Bewley's every morning for coffee for forty years. On the other hand the club atmosphere could sometimes intimidate: on his first day at work in the civil service, young Hugh Leonard *'went at lunchtime to Bewley's in Grafton Street; the noise, the smell of food and the waitresses darting past made him feel like an interloper, and he came out again.'*

1932 was an exciting year for Ireland. The general election in February brought de Valera's Fianna Fáil party to power for the first time, and despite his lack of an overall majority, he at once set about redeeming his election promises. At one level he ushered in an era of republican austerity by refusing to wear a silk top hat on ceremonial occasions, and by declaring that *'no man was worth more than £1,000 a year'* (a view which was unpopular with those heads of the civil service then paid £1,500 a year).

More significantly for Bewley's, he stopped payment of the Land Annuities. These were paid to Britain for land purchased years before by the British government of the day from Anglo-Irish landlords. They amounted to £5 million a year, equivalent to the entire earnings from the export of fat cattle. Britain immediately slapped penal tariffs on Irish imports, and the negative effect on the Irish economy was severe and lasting.

The company which Victor Bewley (joined later by his brothers Alfred

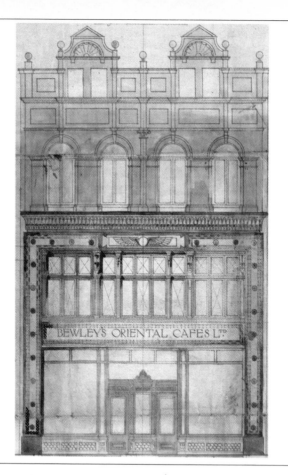

The architect's proposed alterations to 78/9 Grafton Street. Dec. 1925.

and Joseph) took over in 1932 had been established in the social life of Dubliners and visitors for over a generation. It consisted of three premises — George's Street, Westmoreland Street and Grafton Street. Each had a shop and a café, and there were bakeries in Westmoreland Street and Grafton Street supplying the departments, and a 'chocolate factory' (with three employees) also in Westmoreland Street.

Gross takings for 1933, the first full year of Victor's stewardship, were £65,500, on which a pre-tax profit of just under five per cent was made. It was a highly integrated business. Confectionery and rolls made in the firm's bakeries accounted for one-third of the material costs, and butter, milk and cream (largely from the Jersey herd) made up twenty per cent. Coffee and tea together made a further twenty per cent of costs, though this figure greatly understated their contribution to profits. The major overhead expenditure was wages and salaries, which came to just over £17,000, about a quarter of sales.

The shops sold a range of goods, from coffee and tea to tobacco, flowers, Japan ware and pottery, but the key items were the breads and confectionery items (including of course Bewley's famous barm bracks). In Grafton Street these represented nearly sixty per cent of the cost of goods sold. The menu in the cafés on the other hand was narrow by present standards. Coffee and tea, milk, butter, rolls, sticky buns and cakes were the staples, with eggs, sausages and soup. The range had not developed significantly beyond Ernest Bewley's original conception.

Gross Takings by outlet 1933 (£000s)

	Grafton St. £	Westmoreland St. £	George's St £	Total £
Shop	15.9	17.7	5.3	38.9
Café	11.1	13.3	2.2	26.6
Totals	27.0	31.0	7.5	65.5

After only six years in operation, the Grafton Street premises was contributing 40 per cent of the takings, and a gross profit proportionate to the old-established Westmoreland Street premises. On the other hand it had been an expensive conversion, and in return-on-capital terms, Grafton Street was not to break even until the war.

The new managing director had enthusiastic support from all the staff, who were very loyal to the firm and the family, and were no doubt delighted to see someone firmly grasping the tiller again after the two or three years of Ernest Bewley's continuing illness. Victor Bewley relied heavily on the advice of senior staff members such as Theodore Halliday in the general office, Ethel Hewson, who had long been Ernest's personal secretary and was now company secretary, Elizabeth Ward, the manageress of the Grafton Street shop, and Elizabeth Cassidy in the confectionery shop in Westmoreland Street. Another of the stalwarts was Noel Poynton, manager of the Grafton Street café, whose son John became joint managing director many years later.

There was of course no formal consultation, or anything approaching a management committee. As was the style of the time, decision-making powers were kept very clearly in the hands of the Board (that is, the family and its advisors), and only very meagre information about the company was available to anyone else.

At first Victor reported his decisions in detail to the Board. In his report of November 1933, for instance, he agonised over whether to increase the price of coffee. In 1932, he reported, the company had sold 370,000 cups in all, two-thirds at 4 ½d and the rest at 7d; the question was, should he reduce the prices to 4d and 6d? In the end he decided not to.

The first strategic step was to widen the appeal of the cafés: Ernest Bewley had concentrated on providing the very best quality of cakes and other products, at a price, and as a result his market was largely the wealthier classes, the Ascendancy and rich business people. During the twenties many of these people left Ireland, unhappy with the political situation after Independence and the economic outlook for the country, and others were hit by the world recession.

It was clear by 1932 that a new market had to be sought, and with the help of senior staffers, the firm gradually began to phase out the extremely rich and expensive cakes in favour of simpler cakes and buns. The growing business at lunch-time was also catered for by the introduction of snack-type meals. In 1935, evening Whist Drives were promoted, which proved a great success until the lighting restrictions of war made them impossible (in 1988 this tradition was revived with a series of charity Bridge nights); at the same time the idea was mooted of turning one of the upper rooms in Grafton Street into a reading room. A tramway strike in 1935 added to the takings by discouraging people from going home to lunch, and one of the Sweep offices (at least until it was burnt down) provided, as Victor put it in his report, *'a large number of Girls coming for Lunch and Tea'*.

The cumulative effect on turnover of all these developments was marked. By 1936 total takings had gone up to £76,000, and by 1939 they reached £80,000, despite the prevailing economic difficulties.

Considerably more than half of the café turnover came from regulars who could be found at their usual places every day. This was long a feature of Bewley's. When Tommy Webster, one of the small number of Quakers on the staff and a lifetime abstainer, was first manager of Westmoreland Street, he remembers sitting down with his lunch at a table with a group of business-men. Others joined the table, including an acquaintance of his. When the meal was finished his acquaintance took him by the elbow and said: *'Hallo Tommy, I didn't know you were one of us.'* The question was — who were Us? A waitress then told Tommy that the table was filled every day by members of Alcoholics Anonymous. A table in the Grafton Street café was similarly occupied by members of the local Jewish business community.

During these years Bewley's gradually developed its persona as a Dublin club, open to all, and owned in a sense by its customers. The waitresses, simply identified in the wages book by names such as Florrie, Violet, Rose, Gladys, Kitty and Maud, were the key to this relationship. They started work on the dot of nine o' clock, and their first busy time was about eleven as the businessmen came to meet their contacts and take tea or coffee in the Smoke Rooms in Grafton Street and Westmoreland Street. In those days offices tended to be small, uncomfortable and not designed for meetings, so it was quite usual to use cafés for that purpose.

Each waitress had eight tables to look after, and was paid a commission of 2d in the £1 for sales from those tables (plus of course their tips, which were very much their own affair). The commission might amount to an additional ten and fifteen per cent of their wages, which in 1938 varied between 23/- and 30/- a week. As the menu developed this system was to give rise to difficulties. It became increasingly hard for the waitresses to give adequate service to so many tables, yet they were reluctant to give up their favourite customers and the tips they produced, often in pleasantly large lump sums, at Christmas and holiday times. For the not very well paid waitresses, their relationships with regular customers were important, and they took a special pride in serving the many well-known names who frequented the cafés.

Over the year the peaks were the Spring Show, the Horse Show, and Christmas time. One big day was 8 December, a Holy day when by tradition many people came up from the country to do their Christmas shopping, and rounded off the day with a big tea in front of the open fires in the cafés. In the absence of a developed tourist trade, the summer tended to be quite slack. During Lent many customers cut back on buns and cakes in favour of biscuits, and fish was served twice a week.

Tea was still important in the firm's sales, though it had been overtaken by coffee. The price of a pot was fixed at 4½d during most of the thirties. This was the same as a small cup of coffee, but better value, since the pot could be replenished free with extra hot water (a favourite device of students, who could eke out a small pot for many happy hours). The brew was specially blended from several different teas, so that no one leaf dominated. Every year there was an anxious tasting of the new season's samples to ensure that the strong flavour, body, fragrance and leaf appearance the customers demanded was maintained. Experiment was not encouraged: one year the young Victor decided to add the more fragrant early teas too quickly to the blend, only to be overwhelmed by complaints — as he puts it *'the public always assume that any change is for the worse'*. All the tea was brought through the City of London firm of Joseph Travers & Co.

As well as the cafés, there was a delivery service run from the shops. During the 1930s the famous horses, which in Ernest's day had been one of the sights of Dublin, and which still won prizes at the Horse Show, were phased out in favour of motor-vans. The economics of the decision were simple. A horse purchased in 1936 cost £47; a motor van

Mr Ebbett and one of Bewley's famous horses, King's Herald

A range of confectionary products hand crafted at Bewley's chocolate factory.

Oriental vase, such items were once sold in Bewleys.

cost £266. On the other hand *'such a van would do the same work* [as two horses] *more economically, and a considerable amount of extra work in addition.'* In 1937, therefore, the remaining horses were disposed of, a decision that was no doubt regretted a few years later, as the petrol shortages of the war years began to bite.

In September 1939 the Second World War broke out, and the Dáil immediately passed the Emergency Powers Act, which had been drafted and approved by the Cabinet six months before. The immediate effect was a rush to buy up tea and sugar, as consumers quite rightly foresaw shortages of these goods. Bewley's started the Emergency with good stocks of everything, and didn't find it necessary to increase prices. Sales were buoyant, and in 1940 Victor Bewley speculated that one reason for this was that *'a greater number of people have come to live in the city'*. Soon enough, however, the British government restricted shipments of tea first to two ounces a head, then to one and finally to ½ ounce of tea per head.

This was a severe blow for the tea-loving Irish, and for Bewley's. In 1942, for instance, tea purchases by the company accounted for only £364 out of a total of £12,000 worth of food and beverage materials sold in the Westmoreland Street café. In the Grafton Street café tea represented a mere 2.4 per cent of purchases.

Many people shifted their allegiance to coffee, both in cafés and to a much greater extent in the shops. In April 1941 Victor Bewley reported to the board that there were 72 tons in stock, compared to a normal annual sale of 40 tons. Sales of coffee through the shops in 1942 were nearly four times what they had been in 1939. But coffee itself was restricted, and for a while Bewley's supplied a coffee and roasted barley mixture. Then, in 1941 a rather poor quality of coffee from Angola became available, and frustrated tea-drinkers fell on it. In 1949, Victor Bewley reported to the Board that the company had 171 tons of coffee in stock, which then represented about two years' usage. (1987 usage was just under 400 tons.)

Flour was also restricted, and it was made illegal to serve wheaten food twice in a meal. Bewley's therefore experimented with a new range of snacks, such as potato-cakes, oatcakes and scones; custard was used instead of cream. Alfred Bewley organised the cutting of turf straight from the bog — they used 300 tons a year — and Victor Bewley remembers spending much of his time during one damp season stoking the wet turf on to fires in an attempt to get the kettles and the soups boiling in time for the mid-day rush. With the shortage of fuel for transport, for heating and for cooking, more and more people began to use Bewley's in the middle of the day rather than go home. As the menu widened, and more people came to Bewley's for a snack during their restricted lunch-hours, speed of service became important, and more waitresses were employed.

Despite tea rationing, difficulties with coffee supplies and a severe shortage of fuel, the period of the Emergency (as the second world war period was officially called in neutral Ireland) was good for Bewley's.

By the last year of the war, Bewley's turnover had risen to £164,600, sixty per cent of which came through sales in the three shops. The staff was growing, with just under 200 now on the payroll. Individual wages had also risen: the average for waitresses had gone from 27/- per week to 32/-. Despite the decrease in the number of tables served, commissions had doubled from 3/- per week to 6/- on average.

The firm became increasingly valued by the public during the 1940s, as a warm and comfortable haven from the surrounding bleakness and shortages. Not least of the beneficiaries of the Bewley spirit at this time were the hundreds of undernourished children that, with the help of a large group of voluntary helpers, the firm fed after closing time. These had been notified to Professor Collis' Marrowbone Lane Samaritan Fund by hospital almoners as suffering from malnutrition because their normal pre-war diet, which had consisted largely of bread and jam, was cut back by wartime shortages.

When the war ended in 1945 the restrictions it had imposed began gradually to be lifted. But Bewley's customers had caught the café habit (though now demanding more variety), and they continued also their consumption of coffee. As tea became once again readily available, many customers went back to their old favourite, but coffee held others, to such an extent that sales doubled between 1939 and 1946. One thing had been learnt. As soon as possible after the war Victor went to London to buy modern coffee urns to replace the massive old jugs that had previously been used. The regulars, of course, complained bitterly that this new fangled technology was ruining the company, just as they did years later when the urns were replaced in their turn.

As the firm approached the mid-point of the century, the Trustees of Ernest Bewley's estate were able to pay off the last of the debt incurred by the building of Grafton Street. The shares were distributed to his three sons, Victor, Alfred (who had joined the board in 1939), and Joe (1949), and the café leases to his two daughters.

The three brothers were to run the company for the next twenty-seven years, a period in which the economy and the social structure of Ireland was to change radically, to the extent that Bewley's secure position in the marketplace began to be threatened, though at the same time the firm's place in Dubliners' affections grew greater.

CHAPTER FOUR

Troubled Times

'Let's go and have coffee in Bewleys'. The roasting-coffee smell hit one first on the street. An incense that heralded the teak-framed windows filled with fudge, cakes and buns. Pushing through a door into a mahogany-panelled bread-scented warmth, counters of loaves, barmbracks, tea leaves and coffee beans.

Safely here beseated with the years worn on glass-topped tables, dishes mound high with creamy rich butter balls, plates of buns and cream cakes, and the piping hot black cup of aromatic coffee with two little jugs of cream ... in those days Bewley's was comfortably populated with refined mothers and their priest sons. There were, too, accountants, office managers, and the odd shopping elegant housewife. And always in some shadowy corner a hung-over ill-humoured poet would lurk studying the day's racing form. Somehow all these coffee sippers achieved a contentment of sorts out of their temporary reverie and the familiar ministrations of the waitresses ...
J.P. Donleavy

Throughout the 1950s the malaise of an economy in trouble gnawed at the self-respect equally of Dublin's literary men, the journalists in the Palace Bar, the businesspeople, and the civil servants. The rest of Europe was booming, yet every year thousands of people left Ireland, mostly to find work in England. By the end of the 1950s over 400,000 people had gone, from a population at the beginning of the decade of 2.96 million. Senior civil servants such as Dr. T.K. Whitaker, Secretary of the Department of Finance, seriously wondered if the Irish economy could actually operate independently.

In Dublin there was life, at least such as a Monaghan man like Paddy Kavanagh, a Bewley's habitué, might dream of. It was often leisurely (the fastest train between Dublin and Cork in 1948 averaged 37 mph); writers such as Kavanagh, Brendan Behan, Myles na Gopaleen, Anthony Cronin, were much on the streets during the day, and in and out of cafés and pubs, as were others. It is hard now, for instance, to imagine the managing director of a business such as Eason's strolling out of his office twice a day to take refreshments in Westmoreland Street, or the articled clerks in accountants Stokes, Brothers and Pim being allowed to take their afternoon tea in Bewley's.

Bewley's — Dublin's meeting place.

Ernest Bewley and his family take tea in the drawing room of his house in Zion Road, c.1910.

Bewley's was a strictly-run, paternalistic place in these years. In the shops the men had to wear grey or blue suits (no brown was allowed) and shirts with stiff collars, and the waitresses of course wore their black and white uniform, which they supplied themselves. Every morning the doors would be shut at five to nine, so that everyone could be in their place for nine o' clock opening. Any one who was late lost their weekly early-day privilege, or the right to go home at four o' clock.

Victor Bewley knew all his staff and maintained an interest in all of them. In return, despite relatively low rates of pay, they were extremely loyal to him and to the company. He was firm, particularly with offences such as pilfering, but he was often generous. One waitress had been employed only six weeks with the firm before she was diagnosed as having tuberculosis. She was paid her full wages for the year while she was being cured.

Between 1950 and 1960 the firm's turnover grew by 53 per cent, to £390,000, but wages grew disproportionately, so profits only grew just over one-third. Having been 26 per cent of sales in 1933, wages and salaries were now 35 per cent. By 1983 they had soared to 45 per cent. The shops had lost profitability most markedly. They had received an enormous boost during the 1940s, and in 1950 were contributing profits of 20 per cent of turnover to head office; by 1960 this was down to 15 per cent, and the Westmoreland Street shop was down from 21 per cent in 1950 to 14 per cent in 1960.

The management of Bewley's always saw the shops and the cafés as closely integrated. Sales in one area supported those in the other. Ernest Bewley had started coffee making demonstrations and selling rolls to stimulate the retail sales of coffee. However, despite the general image, and the importance of the cafés in social terms, the shops had long been the major part of the business. In fact Bewley's was, and had been for years, a retail business with cafés added, rather than a café business with shops. When the business through the shops faltered, as a result of increasing competition from other retailers, the business as a whole began to falter.

Common to both sides was the famous bakery, at this time split between Grafton Street and Westmoreland Street, in which thirty men produced an endless stream of bracks (2,000 a month), wholemeal bread (400 loaves a day), cherry logs and a host of other favourites. The hundred or more varieties of flans, madeiras, cherry logs, raspberry creams, macaroons, dutch tarts, and lady cakes were all meticulously costed, down to the hundredth of a penny. In 1948 the famous bracks, for instance, cost 9.35d per lb. A 250 lb batch included 72 lbs of flour, 5 lbs of butter, 4 lbs of grapefruit marmalade, 2 gallons of milk, 100 lbs of mixed raisins and sultanas and 16 lbs of peel. Three-quarters of an hour of labour was required to make the mix.

The bakery was Alfred Bewley's special domain. He had served his time under John Swift in the 1930s, and had also spent 1937/8 in a catering school in Leeds. This experience introduced him to substitute products such as Numello (invert sugar) and Panol (emergency fat) which the firm had previously scorned, but was obliged to introduce during the war and immediately afterwards.

In 1960 Joe Bewley joined his brothers Alfred and Victor as joint managing director. Joe was responsible for the farm side, Alfred the bakery, and Victor, the eldest and always the dominant influence, was largely involved in the cafés. The three used to meet at 4.00 p.m. every Monday afternoon in Victor's office to thrash out the affairs of the company. For ordinary staffers and even for younger members of the family, participation in these discussions and subsequent decision-making was slight, and this became something of a grievance during the 1960s.

Commenting on the 1960 accounts, the Chairman of the Board, G.A. Overend of A & L Goodbody, noted *'that the cafe, bakery and farm [profits] were up, while the chocolate factory was down. The increase in wages and salaries was due to a general increase ...'*. For the next few years sales and profits moved slowly up, though in 1965 an improvement in turnover was balanced by a reduction in profits, and this story was repeated in 1967 and 1969.

By this time the new generation of Bewleys had joined the Board, and were starting to make their impact. In 1965 Richard Bewley and John Poynton joined, and in that year Joe Bewley, no doubt prompted by his son Patrick, suggested that a self-service room be introduced for the first time; after a discussion, the decision was deferred.

The firm held fast to the known ways and the basic concept of tea, coffee, chocolates, breads and confectionery. Unfortunately, the clientele was gradually changing. The summer, which had previously been the quiet season when the regulars went on holiday, became vibrant with tourists. Office managers began to supply tea and coffee internally, and to encourage meetings to take place on the premises. Lunches gradually became available from other places, so it no longer became necessary to join the queue for a table in Bewley's, controlled by the porters in their maroon uniforms. Revenue from regulars began to slip below the fifty per cent level.

Other changes were occurring too. The firm began to experience a problem with people slipping past the cash desks without paying their bill. On some days as much as £200 could be lost in this way. A special look-out was kept for these defaulters, and on one occasion Patrick Bewley found himself chased to the door by an irate waitress who hadn't recognised him. In the seventies drug-pushers briefly tried to use the Grafton Street café as a way of contacting local school-girls.

The first reaction to falling profits was to curtail expenditure (in 1966 the Board minutes recorded that '*Mr Poynton explained the advantages of having an internal telephone system, but in view of costs it was decided to leave it for the moment*'), and to raise prices: a cup of coffee went up to 11d (small) and 1/2d (large) in 1967. This was three times the price charged in 1932: in the same period average industrial earnings had gone from just over £125 pa to £820.

In January 1968 Victor Bewley calculated that the effect of a further penny on a cup of coffee would increase turnover by £5,000, and 3d on soup by £2,340. The full list of price increases suggested gives a good idea of the menu of the time: an extra £17,000 sales was to be raised by increases on milk, toast, chips, puddings, beans, eggs, chops, sausages, peas, baked pies, cakes and butter. These increases gave a welcome relief in 1968, but the following year decline set in again. In March Victor Bewley noted that the public had reacted unfavourably to recent price increases, and '*as well as this there was an increase in wages*'.

In October 1968 a general Board discussion on the future development of the company took place, in which the younger members (including by now Patrick Bewley) urged some radical initiatives. The rapid development of the city suburbs presented both a threat and an opportunity. This trend, which had worked to Bewley's benefit in previous decades, now began to threaten its existence. As suburban centres developed more sophisticated shopping facilities, it no longer became necessary to go into town to shop, and both the shops and the cafés suffered in consequence. Patrick Bewley was authorised to bid for the lease interest in a shop in Dublin's first suburban shopping centre in Stillorgan.

The first self-service area, on the second floor in Grafton Street, was opened in December 1969. The columnist Quidnunc lamented both the

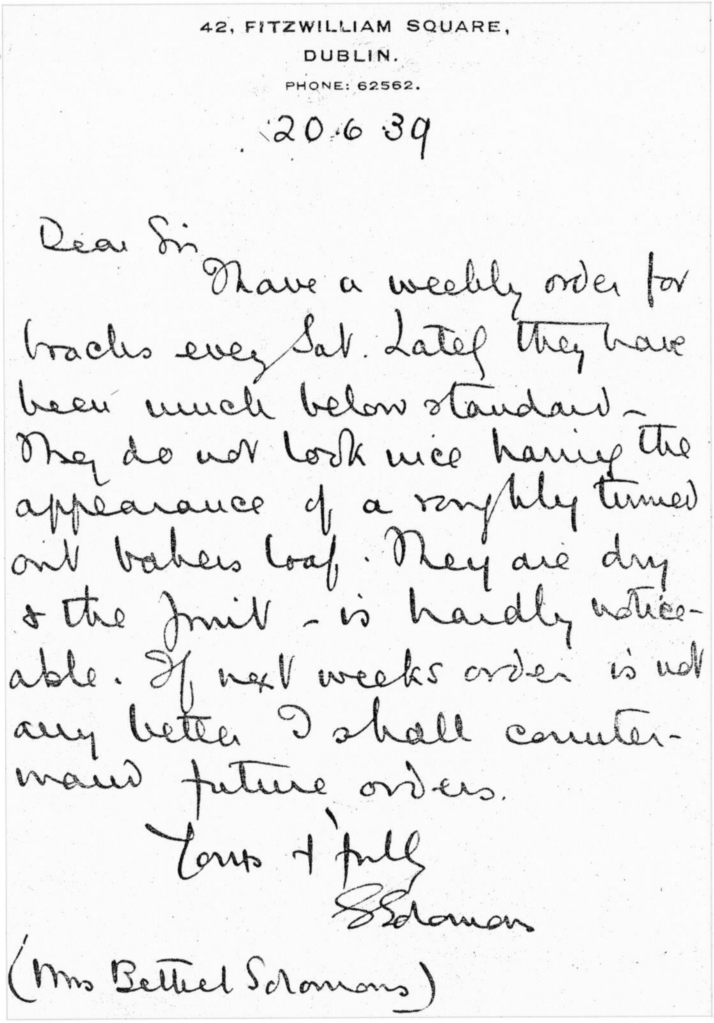

42, FITZWILLIAM SQUARE,
DUBLIN.
PHONE: 62562.

20.6 39

Dear Sir
I have a weekly order for bracks every Sat. Lately they have been much below standard. They do not look nice having the appearance of a roughly turned out bakers loaf. They are dry + the fruit - is hardly notice-able. If next weeks order is not any better I shall counter-mand future orders.

Yours + fully
SSolomon

(Mrs Bethel Solomons)

Mrs. Solomons husband Bethel, a famous gynaecologist, appears in Finnegans Wake.

change to self-service, and the opening-up of the men-only Smoke Room downstairs: *'the club room where grave men from every walk of Dublin life resolved the fate of the nation every morning since the turn of the century has this week been taken from them ... the wrought-iron pot-bellied stove which dominated the alcoved booths and the mahogany coat-racks have already gone. So has the service counter from which bacon and eggs, rolls various, meringues and the best coffee in Ireland has been dispensed for years by young waitresses whose terms of employment, it would seem, required them to join the firm with an inbuilt sense of motherliness.'* (*The Irish Times* October 1970).

The spread of self-service undoubtedly helped the firm to cut down on its wages bill, which had mounted to an alarming degree. On the other hand perhaps Dubliners were for once right to complain about an innovation. The waitresses were very close to the customers in the way that self-service staff never can be, and this was valued by both sides. When the bond was cut, something seems to have been lost to

The shop in Westmoreland Street before the disastrous fire in 1977.

the company.

At the beginning of the 1970s the company was actively seeking new markets, and struggling, reasonably successfully, with increasing inflation. Partly due to the contribution from the Stillorgan shop, which was a success from its opening in May 1970, the results in 1972 showed a considerable improvement on previous years. This was the background to a radical experiment in industrial democracy which was to occupy much of the company's energies over the 1970s and 1980s.

Victor Bewley had been concerned about the long-term ownership of the company for some time. As managing director, he frequently saw applicants for jobs, and he became struck by the impact of a recent spate of take-overs. One day he asked an applicant: *'why did you leave your previous position?'* *'The firm was sold and I became redundant,'* she said. *'How long had you been there?'*, he continued. *'Over thirty years,'* was her reply.

He and his brothers felt that the staff should be given more control in two areas: firstly in the ownership of the capital, which at that time rested in very few hands, and secondly in participation in discussion and decision-making. Eventually, after a meeting of all the members of the family involved in the business, it was decided that the shares be transferred to a guarantee company called The Bewley Community. This would be controlled by nine trustees, made up of three staff appointees, three directors' appointees and three outsiders appointed jointly by the community and the directors. They had specific rights to veto any measure taken by the Directors if they felt that the measure *'would involve a breach of the principles upon which the company is constituted'* as the Articles put it. This right was in fact never exercised.

All members of staff with more than three years service could apply to become members of the Community. The idealistic principles of the Community were taken into account in a revision of the company's Articles, which were changed to read:

2. *The organs of the Company ... shall have regard at all times to the fact that the basic purpose of the Company is to render the best possible service as a body corporate to the Community and to encourage thinking in terms of the welfare of the Community in which we live, rather than a desire for personal gain at the cost of others. Toward this end, capital should be used to serve the needs of human beings, not the reverse, and the operations of the Company will be directed to:*

(i) *producing goods and services not only beneficial to the customers of the Company at fair prices and of as high a quality as possible, but also for the general good of mankind.*

(ii) *providing economic security for employees of the Company.*

(iii) *developing the strength of the Company, its efficiency and organisation and*

(iv) *contributing towards the general welfare of society.*

3. *For the aforementioned purposes the organs of the Company shall take such measures as they think fit and in particular:*

(i) *Direct the affairs of the Company so that the employees may fully participate in the Company's activities in relation to their ability, knowledge and experience, so as to create a fellowship of people working together for a common goal, and ...*

(iii) *prepare the Company's accounts in conformity with the principles governing the Company.*

It is recognised as a desirable principle that members of the Company should on all occasions endeavour to reach a unanimous decision without need for a formal vote. The procedures for voting which are laid down are only intended to be used as a last resort.

These constitutional developments took place during a time of rapid change in the company. In 1972 turnover exceeded £1 million for the first time, and pre-tax profit stood at £59,000. The following year turnover was up, profits down. In that year the the first non-family board members were appointed; Beatrice Lunney, the cafe manageress in Grafton Street, who had joined the firm before the war as a shop assistant, and Brendan Mealy, from the bakery, joined seven Bewleys at the top of the company.

By 1975 the company's cash flow problems were worsening, and the board asked the staff to postpone the 8 per cent national wage agreement for six months, when it would be backdated; only those who requested it (about 10 per cent) were paid immediately. In June 1977 Victor and his brothers retired from their positions as joint managing directors, and Richard Bewley, John Poynton and Patrick Bewley were appointed in their place.

Article 3 (i) was put into practice by establishing a staff Council to discuss matters relating to the business. It consisted of heads of departments and elected representatives, amounting to 45 people in all, out of over 400 staff. The Council was made as undaunting as possible, but it was still a large gathering, and it took some time before its working style became established, although it was a popular forum from the beginning. By 1977 however, the year of Victor's retirement, it was off the ground.

A selection of morning products from Bewley's Bakery, featuring the traditional barm brack in the foreground.

A Chinese lacquered tea bin, until recently used in the shops, now on display in the Bewley Museum, Grafton Street.

In November of that year, the Council was informed that over 19,000 bracks had been produced and sold for Hallowe'en, an increase of 1,000 on the previous year. The new shop in Dun Laoghaire had sold almost 2,000. This good news was tempered by the announcement that there was a loss of £53,000 for the first eight months of the year, and that coffee sales were dropping, despite an attempt earlier in the year to push sales of a coffee and barley mix. Takings for the Christmas period were expected to be £535,000 out of a total annual sales of £2.4 million. These figures were worse than might have been expected, partly as a result of a disastrous fire in Westmoreland Street, which, apart from destroying many of the company's records, cost thousands in lost sales.

The Council met once every two months or so, and its agenda generally started with a report on sales by outlet. This was often followed by details from the profit and loss account. At this time the management were keen to develop new lines in the cafés and information about these was often given at this point. (The extreme conservatism of the Irish café-goer always made new lines risky — Beatrice Lunney describes how she occasionally bullied her regulars into ordering a new lunch snack. 'Well', they would typically respond, '*it was very nice, but I think I'll stick to my usual in future.*') Reports from the departments followed, and then suggestions from the representatives on a wide variety of matters such as holiday priority, Easter Saturday opening, a children's menu and so on. Management representatives frequently took the opportunity to urge such matters as hygiene standards, attention to detail and morale.

Despite its high ideals, the Council was not able to provide the leadership in difficult times the staff were looking for. One reason for this was a vagueness, even among the representatives elected by departments, as to its powers. Because they had been consulted about the details of the pension scheme, some believed that the Council was a decision-making body. This was wrong. The Council was simply a vehicle for communication, and didn't even exist legally in the company's articles. Its only power was as a persuasive force on the Trustees of The Bewley Community, who were the ultimate owners of the company.

In June 1979 Christy Fox, Chairman of the Community Council, commented that staff did not really see the relevance of the Council to them, so they were not really interested in it. The power vacuum was rapidly filled by the unions, whose members in April 1980 staged a walk-out in Westmoreland Street on the grounds that they no longer wished to work with non-unionised staff. In the Community Council meeting that discussed the situation, Christy Fox somewhat unsympathetically remarked that those who walked out '*were shareholders of the firm and that they should be more concerned with the figures and trying to increase our sales...*'. The same year, at a Council meeting with the Board, Fox regretted a '*growing aggressiveness in the younger staff who were unionised. As a result staff who were not in the union felt ... that the Management was not reacting positively in relation to the advent of unions in the shop and cafés.*'

These were symptoms of an unhappy company, and soon absenteeism

The Diceman, Tom McGinty, promoting Bewley's Easter Eggs.

began to be a problem. In February 1980, for instance, it was pointed out to the Council that in the first seven weeks of the year nearly 1,200 days had been lost through absenteeism. One staff member in twelve was absent every day. Beatrice Lunney discovered by accident the reason for at least one absence. She called in for tea to a rival café, and was served by one of her own staff. As Miss Lunney put it *'the girl was so surprised to see me she nearly dropped the tray in my lap!'*

The company entered the 1980s in a troubled mood. Company Chairman Patrick Bewley reported to the Annual General Meeting on 28 May 1980 that sales had gone up to over £3 million, but pre-tax profits were below 1 per cent, considerably less than the bankers were looking for. The Board however felt it desirable to pay a staff bonus of £16 a head, for the first time since 1973. Patrick Bewley also reported that free meals were available to all staff, as well as increased holidays, and hoped that the *'bond of friendship'* could be reactivated, and that *'we will all work together towards making our company healthier, wealthier but above all happier.'* The next few years were to show that this was not going to be easy to achieve.

CHAPTER FIVE

Crisis

I entered Bewley's at twenty to nine and took my place on a red-cushioned seat. 'Large coffee and almond buns, please.' I relaxed with the morning's greeting from the old lady with the blue coat and hat pin. As is customary, she then advised me as to which picture to see — today she suggested a Western at the Ambassador Cinema — based on what the head usher has told her in each of the cinemas. She knows all of the ushers by name, and they her ... I sat back in the cushioned seat, postponing the slide into the morning paper ... in Bewley's Oriental Cafés you are bound to see someone you would like to be with, someone you are glad you are not with, and someone you wish you had something of in you. Philip Davison *The Book-Thief's Heartbeat* (1981)

The firm's great asset was the enormous amount of affection and goodwill its customers had for it. Between 40,000 and 45,000 visited the cafés every week, looking for the best coffees in town, and for a familiar, much-loved scene. Dubliners love people, and from the security of one's table the passing show, garnished with a suitable proportion of eccentrics, could be enjoyed to the full.

The dramatic developments in the internal constitution of the company made Bewley's nationally and internationally famous. In publications as diverse as *The Word* and *The Financial Times* articles were written praising The Bewley Community as an experiment in industrial relations, and describing its operations.

Unfortunately in practice the situation was not as rosy as it might have been. The older staff remained extremely loyal to the Bewley family, especially to Victor, but the younger employees were less impressed by the spirit of the Community. In 1982 an American student of industrial relations surveyed the staff, and discovered that 80 per cent wanted more information about Bewley's, and 70 per cent more job information. Two-thirds of the staff seldom or never spoke to their supervisors about job ideas.

'Tattins' Twomey has been a waitress in Grafton Street for nearly forty years.

Barney Johnson, a baker, was Chairman of The Bewley Community up to 1986, and 36 years with the company.

Even if the experiment had been a triumphant success, the problems facing the company were not to be solved in this way. Indeed, although the Council certainly enabled changes such as the widespread introduction of self-service to go through without creating a residue of bitterness, it distracted the management from its task of re-creating the viability of the company. The key problem was described by Company Secretary John Thompson in a memo: *'Bewley's used to have a niche, possibly up to the early 1970s. Since then the world has changed and we haven't found a new place in the market. Who are our customers?'*

The second problem, which ultimately prevented the first from being solved, was the annual pension bill. When Victor took over the company in 1932 there was no formal retirement age or pension scheme. Pensions were provided in special circumstances by special decision. Thus when the horses were phased out in 1937, the Board agreed that the two redundant men (one of whom had been with the company for 42 years) be given a pension of 15/- a week (plus 10/- if married). Two years later the Board was told that *'since neither of these men is yet eligible for the Old Age Pension'* the arrangement would be continued for a further year.

From the 1940s £450 was put away each year to the Pension fund reserve, which by 1960 had accumulated to a capital sum of £18,500; the total cost of pensions in that year was £2,700.

By the time the Community was set up in 1972, a full blown pension scheme was in action, with automatic pensions for retired staff and their widows. The annual contribution to the pension fund had not been increased, unfortunately, so pensions were now being paid largely out of current earnings. As long as the company prospered this could be done, but in lean times the pension commitment became a serious burden. A hint of what might happen occurred in 1974, when Victor and his Board generously increased pension benefits — and at the same time the company recorded its second annual loss since incorporation in 1927. The lack of a funded pension scheme was to have serious repercussions in the crisis years of the 1980s.

The pension commitment and a faltering market position were hard enough problems to solve, but in the early 1980s they were joined by external threats. The company was hit hard by the economic recession that started in 1979, and by the rapidly increasing VAT levels. Customers did not increase their spending, so the company lost out. Each new problem reduced the decision-space for the others. Although turnover doubled to £5.2 million between 1977 and 1983, by that time trading losses had mounted to £4,000 a week.

Throughout the 1980s, the Board wrestled with these problems, trying various means to re-establish the company's profits and to avoid an end which began to seem increasingly inevitable. Senior management was changed (several times), new product lines introduced, cost-reduction schemes initiated, more self-service was imposed on the cafes and franchising was developed. Somehow it seemed that the steps that might have saved the situation eluded them. Perhaps this was because the unique corporate culture, with its humane bias, prevented the hard decisions being taken. Work practices and staff levels were probably too indulgent. The culture also seemed to make it difficult to enforce standards, and the level of quality began to fall off, a fact that the customers were not slow to notice, and to complain of. The 150 or so different items produced by the bakery were particularly variable in quality.

Like heroes in a Greek tragedy, the protagonists seemed powerless to extricate themselves from the firm's past. In February 1982 the Board asked, with a touch of despair, 'How long will there be a need for our company?', and, 'Why do we assume we are doing things correctly? Is there a better way?'. In May of that year, facing another loss, the 'apparent ineffectiveness of the Board was discussed', but to little effect. Two months later it was reported that it was only possible to keep within the company's overdraft limits by putting off certain payments to creditors. This decision, taken under pressure, was later to have dramatic consequences.

In 1983, the Board appointed an external consultant, Aidan Barry of O'Hare Barry & Co. He produced a report on the company which

A variety of Bewley's and othe[r] Irish products go into one of th[e] 5,000 Christmas hampers sold b[y] Bewleys every year.

The Fleet Street café was originally intended for a bicycle repair shop.

Self-service was gradually introduced throughout the 1970s.

identified a series of problems, some of which, such as the extreme involvement of senior executives in operational detail, were deliberate matters of management style. He described the employees as having been *'protected too long from the commercial realities of the outside world'*. Suggestions were made for developing the franchise operation, for selling assets, and of course for more marketing and public relations, but they scarcely seemed to approach the real problem. Barry was to be intimately involved in the gathering crisis of the company's affairs over the next few years.

One bright spot in the company was the very successful creation of the Catering and Wholesale division in 1979. This was timed to meet the continuing demand for coffee, Irish sales of which tripled between 1960 and 1984. Before this all coffee orders for individual customers, and also for large users such as Trinity College, had all been fulfilled at the counter in the shop. Completing the Trinity order might take an attendant several hours, subject always to interruptions by walk-in customers. This was obviously not efficient for the large customers or the small. Patrick Bewley therefore set up and led this new division, whose turnover went from £300,000 in the first year to nearly double that two years later.

Following the consultant's advice the farm was sold in 1984, which eased the cash flow situation, but losses continued to mount. With the losses, difficulties proliferated. In October members of the ITGWU complained to the Labour Court about the deferment of payments of the 23rd Round of the National Pay Agreement. The Board noted that to pay these amounts would constitute *'an impossible financial burden on the company'*.

The continuing difficulties, and the fact that the problems remained so long unresolved, worried and frustrated the staff. As staff morale dropped, service tended to suffer. Journalist Kevin Myers described the result: *'for us devotees of Bewley's, life was not always easy. We would creep in on tip-toes so as not to give offence to the workforce — that is the waitresses — who were normally busy talking ... all around would be unfed, unrefreshed patrons of Bewley's, all waiting in obeisant silence for one or other of the waitresses to break up their little parliament. While we waited we would exchange meek little smiles, like timorous adherents to a cult waiting for the high priest to begin.'*

A new managing director was appointed in January 1985 to activate a rescue plan. His general strategy, after three years of mounting losses, was based on *'trading our way out of the present difficulties ...'*. Once again the radical solution (if such a thing was possible) eluded the company. Four months later he had resigned and was replaced by the finance director, Sean Sheehan. The Board then spent a marathon session of eighteen hours in a general review of the company's operation in April 1985, with a view to preparing a submission to Foir Teo, the state-sponsored body that provides rescue finance to industrial companies in danger of closing down. The core of the problem was clearly identified as the cafés. These, incidentally, were now referred to as restaurants, in an attempt to persuade the customer to spend more money per visit.

Foir Teo turned down the company's request for help in August 1985, and the Board noted *'that in spite of all the efforts of recent years the Company did not have a viable future without a radical rethink and change of direction.'* By the end of the year losses were running at the rate of £10,000 a week, and the first approach had been made to a government department for help. The last act of the drama had begun.

In May 1986 Patrick Bewley, Chairman of the company, sombrely addressed the sixtieth annual general meeting. *'It gives me,'* he said, *'no pleasure to report once again that our company has incurred a substantial loss for the year. Despite all our efforts and changes, we still incurred a loss of £418,000 for the year ended 31 January 1986. Redundancy and retirement costs of £133,000 are included in this figure ... In the last few weeks we have examined the various options open to us, from an association with another firm to closing down completely. The closing down option was the least attractive, as that leaves only statutory redundancy for staff and very little or nothing for pensioners.'* The 140 pensioners, who had already had their pensions reduced by one-third earlier in the year, now faced the possibility of losing them altogether.

Although this announcement came as no surprise to the staff, who, through the Council were well-informed of the state of affairs, Dubliners were shocked by An Taoiseach Garret Fitzgerald's revelation on the day of the AGM that Bewley's were in difficulties. Prompted by Joan Fitzgerald, a life-long patron of the Grafton Street shop, Garret Fitzgerald said that he had *'taken a close interest in the company's problems, and that because Bewley's was a national asset, and one of Dublin's best-loved institutions that meant a lot to a lot of people'*, he had urged the hotel and tourism training body CERT to help out. Patrick Bewley described himself as *'surprised and delighted'* by this intervention.

Behind the scenes, negotiations had already been going on with various potential purchasers of the firm, including the hotelier P.V. Doyle. One of these purchasers told Albert Reynolds (then opposition spokesman on industry) who made it public, that the firm by now owed the Revenue Commissioners about £1 million in deferred PAYE/PRSI and VAT payments. Reynolds, a Roscommon man, took the view that there were objects more deserving of government help than a Dublin café company that had failed to pay its due to the Revenue. This debt, which actually amounted to £926,000, was more than enough to sink the company.

By August 1986 it was clear to the Board that there were three serious options: to find a purchaser, to sell various substantial sections of the cafés and other assets, or to go into liquidation. Garret Fitzgerald's announcement, though it had not in the end resulted in any action from state organisations, had flushed out several possible buyers from the private sector. These included two property agencies, several coffee firms (whose main interest was in the thriving Catering and Wholesale division), a bakery company and a catering firm. It eventually became clear that the most serious of these was Campbell Catering, run by 44 year-old Patrick Campbell.

In the mid-1960s, Patrick Campbell and his wife Veronica had started, after training in the Dublin College of Catering and abroad, to cater for private parties and planned-giving functions in Dublin. One of these involved catering for the 6,000 people that Archbishop McQuaid had invited to contribute to the pro-cathedral. Campbell Catering Ltd was established in 1967. The firm's first big contract was to supply 35,000 sandwiches a day to Dublin schools; from that the company grew rapidly until by 1986 it had sales of over £15 million. It employed over 600 people all over the country, feeding 20,000 people daily in venues as diverse as Dublin Zoo, offshore rigs, University College Cork, Irish Distillers and Bord Telecom.

When Bewley's problems hit the headlines, the company had been planning to expand into Britain, possibly with a chain of restaurants. Both executive time and cash was therefore available to be swung behind Bewley's. On the other hand Bewley's, though the cafes and shops were familiar territory for Campbells, had important ingredients such as the wholesale coffee business and the bakery about which they knew much less. The first approach, in June 1986, was therefore tentative. Campbell himself even went to the United States in July, having decided that Bewley's problems were intractable. Negotiations at this stage were handled by his managing director Lorraine Sweeney, who continued to play a key role in subsequent developments.

By 7 October 1986 the Bewley Board finally agreed that there was no internal solution (for instance by selling assets) that was both credible and widely acceptable. The Revenue Commissioners had agreed in September that they would hold off the registration of the judgement for £926,000 owed by the company until 7 November. Although it might have been possible to extend that date, no potential purchaser would choose to negotiate with that risk hanging over them, for as soon as the Revenue did register the amount, the company would have to be wound up.

An immediate purchaser was therefore essential, and the Campbell Catering offer seemed the most promising. This amounted to £5.5 million, made up of £2.5 million for liabilities (which were almost exactly balanced by the value of the assets), £1 million for the Revenue, £1 million to guarantee existing and future pensions, and a £1 million investment programme. It was an offer for the whole business as a going concern, to be carried on, as the offer document put it, *'in the tradition and style which has made the company synonymous with the best qualities of Dublin life'*. On 8 October the Board decided to recommend the Campbell Catering offer to the shareholders.

In order to finalise the sale, various groups had to agree. Firstly there was the Board, which had already accepted the offer; then there were the Bewley Community Trustees, who accepted the Board's view; finally there were the five unions, whose members made up the majority of the shareholders of the Bewley Community, the ultimate owners of the company. Their interest was to get the best possible pay and conditions for their members. Out of the argument altogether were the pensioners, who could be said to have had most hanging on the result.

The unusual ownership structure of Bewley's made it difficult at first for Campbells to identify where the power lay. It also made it essential to get the workers' consent to the purchase. Campbells therefore spent a lot of time going round the various departments explaining their proposals in detail. They had to be satisfied that, if they took over Bewley's, the unions would not be able to serve large subsequent claims on them. An Extraordinary General Meeting of The Bewley Community to approve the sale was arranged for 4 November, a few days before the expiry of the Revenue's moratorium. By the end of October, however, negotiations between the unions and Campbell Catering were still in difficulties. The deadline set by the Revenue was coming perilously close.

About 150 members of staff attended the meeting on Tuesday 4 November. The unions still believed that the pay and conditions implicit in the Campbell Catering offer could be improved on, and so all the unions involved, except the Bakers, advised their members to reject the offer. Their members put this into effect by adjourning the EGM *'to allow more time for negotiations between Campbell Catering and the trade unions.'* After further discussions, at which it was clear that no agreement was likely to be reached, Campbell Catering formally withdrew their offer on 5 November.

The *Evening Herald* reported (on the front page): *'The famous Bewley's restaurant chain is on the brink of closure following workers' rejection of a take-over deal. The threat of closure came following the decision by café workers, maintenance workers and shop staff to turn down the takeover terms offered*

By KATHERINE DONNELLY, Industrial Correspondent

THE famous Bewleys restaurant chain was on th
brink of closure today following workers' rejec
tion of a takeover deal.

Frantic efforts to get the workers — who are also share
holders — to change their minds failed this morning.

The threat of closure came following
decision last night by cafe assistants, maintena
workers and shop staff to turn down the takee
terms offered by Campbell Catering.

by Campbell Catering.' This was, as John Thompson put it, 'our lowest point'.

The resumed meeting of the Bewley Community on the evening of Thursday 6 November was told that the offer had been withdrawn, and that 'in the circumstances the Company would have no option but to cease trading ...'. A further adjournment was sought, and the following day the unions delivered a shopping basket of new claims to Campbells, including requests for free meals, and greater wage increases. In Campbells' view this mixture of brinkmanship, misunderstanding of the seriousness of the situation, and an attempt to do better for their members was simply too late. They had withdrawn their offer, and were interested only in clarifying its terms. Union officials rejected this, and declined to reconvene their members.

The final session of the EGM, on the evening of Friday 7 November, began in an almost unbearably tense atmosphere. After more hours of talks, the position was still deadlocked; this was the last possibility of saving the company from bankruptcy. At 6.30 the remaining customers were bustled out of the Westmoreland Street café, and the staff, pensioners and union representatives (who had been invited by the Board) assembled. The waiting newspaper and radio reporters heightened the sense of history being made. The Board decided that Aidan Barry, as the only outside director, should put its view to the staff.

At this stage the younger café workers stood out most strongly against the deal, wanting particularly pay increases, a larger free meal allowance

But Bewleys directors asked Campbell Catering
·lay a final decision on withdrawing their £2
on takeover offer while attempts were made to
staff agreement.

The offer was finally withdrawn at 11 a.m. today.

Now the Campbell Catering offer has gone, closure
s almost certain for the 146-year-old firm loved by
ations of Dubliners.

Taoiseach, Dr. Garret FitzGerald, has described
eys as an "integral and vital part of Dublin's essen-
character and atmosphere, which should be pre-
·d as far as possible".

'Our lowest point'
*— the firm on the brink of
collapse. The front page of the
Evening Herald, Nov. 6, 1986.*

and different work rosters. They ranged themselves in a solid group
at the back of the Fleet Street room. Barry explained in detail what would
happen if the Campbell offer was rejected. To a highly emotional
gathering, he described how the liquidator would go about brutally
dismantling the 140-year-old firm in which so many of them had made
their lives. Even if buyers could be found for some of the cafés, he said,
it was probable that they would refuse to employ existing staff. The
pensioners would face penury — were the young waitresses going to
deprive the old people of their pensions?

The union members requested an adjournment, and then another,
and then another. They went into huddles among themselves, each
union separately, while the Board, the pensioners and the non-union
staff (some 60 in all) sat — tense, distressed, numb, a few even crying
— and waited. The meeting resumed at 8.20, and was adjourned until
8.50; further adjournments were asked for and granted.

At last the union officials secured an agreement to an aggregate secret
ballot of all union members. This brought an 87-29 vote in favour of the
Campbell proposals. With the non-union votes and the Bakers', the yes-
vote now had a comfortable majority. It was left only for Patrick Bewley
to contact Patrick Campbell (waiting in Bloom's Hotel) and tell him of
the result. The union members' acceptance enabled him to renew
Campbell Catering's offer to buy Bewley's, which he did. The formalities
were over by 11.30, and the meeting stumbled out into a pouring wet
night.

BEWLEY'S TODAY

For most people, the events of November 1986 meant that Bewley's had been saved from extinction. When Patrick Campbell took over as Chairman of the firm on 1 December, however, he was in no doubt that the rescue was only just beginning.

The lack of profitability in recent years had allowed little or nothing to be spent on replacing or refurbishing equipment and buildings. The extent of this only became clear after Campbells took over, and the capital expenditure budget was quickly revised upwards to £3.8 million.

Part of this expenditure was funded by the sale and leaseback of the Grafton Street premises to the Royal Insurance Company for £2.9 million in 1987. Refurbishment of the company's flagship, at a cost of £1.5 million, commenced immediately afterwards, and the restoration work was fully completed early in 1988. By then franchising of Bewley's cafés and shops had been confirmed as a major growth area for the firm, in Ireland, in Britain and in North America.

Patrick Bewley continued successfully with the firm, and became Managing Director of a new subsidiary, Bewley's Tea & Coffee Ltd in January 1988. This company took over the activities of the old Catering and Wholesale division. Since the take-over, the antiquated coffee roasters, grinders and other ancillary equipment have all been replaced, and this has provided production capacity for Bewley's to become the market leader for ground coffee in Ireland.

Bewley's tea carried its distinctive taste and quality into the 1980s, but it needed to be packaged and marketed in a positive and professional manner. A range of new packaging was designed, a marketing drive undertaken, and in 1988 tea sales had doubled and were expected to double again in 1989. Today, Bewley's tea is to be found on the shelves of leading department and speciality stores in the major cities of Europe and North America, where it has begun to displace some of the best known brands.

In the autumn of 1987 Bewley's bakery was transferred to Dublin's Portland Street where it was combined with the chocolate factory, which had previously been located in Grafton Street. The now famous Bewley's Museum was housed in the old chocolate factory. Portland Street provided increased scope for the production of breads, cakes and confectionery in a splendid new environment, using the traditional recipes which had made them famous. The enormous amount of time and effort which had earlier been devoted to design, packaging, and marketing these products, was beginning to show dividends by the second half of 1988. In fact, the demand for products such as shortbread,

To celebrate   1988 Dublin Millenium, Bewley's baked this enormous Viking ship cake: Lord Mayor Ben Briscoe enjoys the first slice.

fruitcake and Christmas puddings in both home and export markets grew to the extent that production of other famous Bewley's products such as almond rings and Mary cakes was temporarily suspended.

Following the takeover there were fears that friction might develop between the new management and the workers (who had previously owned the firm). In practice, most of the workers found themselves better off as a result. They received three pay increases over the eighteen months after 1986 which compared well with no pay increases in the two years prior to the takeover. Also, there was a voluntary redundancy scheme for those who wished to opt out (about 50 did so).

The new owners however could not continue to invest in aspects of the business which did not offer the prospect of a viable return. For this reason the trading results from the refurbished Grafton Street and Stillorgan premises would have an important bearing on the future of Bewley's cafés and shops. It was clear that these retail outlets needed not just substantial investment, but a tremendous degree of commitment to customers by staff and management alike.

Various training and development programmes were implemented during 1987 and 1988 for staff at all levels, to improve the quality of products and services. Minds were concentrated on the changes, and on the work to be done. There was a new singularity of purpose in the firm.

Whatever changes took place, it was important that Bewley's should always retain that character, that tradition, for which it had become revered. This it has done. On the day that café in Grafton Street re-opened after the completion of an eight-week £1.5 million refurbishment programme in March 1988, Patrick Campbell stood in the hall, nervously awaiting the reaction of the early morning patrons. Among the first to enter was a customer of long-standing, who scrutinised the café with a beady eye, stamped his foot, and complained loudly 'I don't know why you had to lock us out for the last two months — you haven't changed anything!'

The Board after the take-over in 1986: (from left) Patrick Bewley, Patrick Campbell, Lorraine Sweeney, Paddy Kelly.

INDEX

ACKNOWLEDGEMENTS

This book is based on three sources of information: firstly and most illuminatingly, the memories of people who worked in the firm and their customers, in particular Aidan Barry, Alfred Bewley, Mary Bewley, Patrick Bewley, Victor Bewley, Patrick Campbell, Beatrice Lunney, John Swift, John Thompson and Tommy Webster, all of whom gave generously of their time and knowledge.

Historical insights and references came from Dr. E. M. Crawford, Dr. David Dickson and Peter Pearson, the organiser of the Bewley museum in Grafton Street.

The second source is the various written documents that survived the fire in Westmoreland Street in 1977, in particular the Minutes of Board Meetings and other similar documents. These include annual accounts, reports, internal memoranda, minutes of Council meetings, wages books, bakery costing sheets and so on. They are identified in the text when referred to specifically, but even when not, they have formed the backbone of the story.

The third source is in published documents. These range from ephemeral articles in the daily press to parliamentary reports. The main books used were:

E. T. Bewley *The Bewleys of Cumberland and their Irish and other descendants* (Dublin 1920)

British Parliamentary Papers: *Report of the Select Committee on Tea Duties* (1834)

— *Report of the Select Committee on Industries (Ireland)* (1885)

— *Report on Financial relations between Ireland and England* (1897)

L. Cullen: *The Emergence of Modern Ireland 1700-1900* (Dublin 1981)

M. Daly *The Famine in Ireland* (Dublin 1986)

R. Ellmann *Letters of James Joyce* (London 1966)

D. Forrest *Tea for the British* (London 1973)

R. Harrison *Dublin Quakers in business 1800-1850* (unpublished M.Litt thesis TCD 1988)

H. Leonard *Home Before Night* (London 1979)

D. McMahon *The Irish Quaker Community 1870-1925* (unpublished M.A. thesis, UCD 1985)

E. Malcolm *Ireland sober, Ireland free* (Dublin 1986)

D. Norris *Joyce's Dublin* (Dublin 1982)

J. O'Brien *"Dear, Dirty Dublin"* (California 1982)

H. Oram *Bewleys* (Dublin 1978)

J. Robins *Fools and Mad* (Dublin 1986)

B. Share *The Emergency* (Dublin 1978)

Statistical Abstract (various years)

F. Tobin *The Best of Decades* (Dublin 1984)

PHOTOGRAPHY

Ameila Stein; *8, 11, 12, 17, 20.* The Irish Architectural Archives; *22, 23.* Ameila Stein; *25.* Liam O'Leary Archives; *27.* The National Gallery of Ireland; *27.* Ameila Stein; *32, 41, 44.* Eddie de Barra; *50.* Ameila Stein, *53.* Eric Luke; *53.* Emila Stein; *56, 58, 60, 61, 62.* Liam Blake; *68;* Peter Zoellar; *70.*